THE PICTURE LIFE OF

# FRANKLIN DELANO
# ROOSEVELT

THE PICTURE LIFE OF

# FRANKLIN DELANO
# ROOSEVELT

by SAM and BERYL EPSTEIN

*illustrated with photographs*

FRANKLIN WATTS, INC.
575 LEXINGTON AVENUE
NEW YORK, N.Y. 10022

PHOTOGRAPHS COURTESY OF:
United Press International, pages 12, 45, 50, 52, 62.
Wide World, pages 20, 60.
The balance of the photographs were used with the permission
of the Franklin D. Roosevelt Library, Hyde Park, New York.

# THE PICTURE LIFE OF
# FRANKLIN DELANO
# ROOSEVELT

President Franklin Delano Roosevelt, June 29, 1938.

Franklin Delano Roosevelt was the only man
ever elected President of the United States
four times.
Many people believe he was one of the
nation's greatest Presidents.

Franklin Delano Roosevelt was born on
    January 30, 1882, at Hyde Park, New York.
    His father, James Roosevelt, was a
    well-to-do businessman. The Roosevelts
    were a proud old New York family. The
    first Roosevelt had come to America from
    Holland in about 1636.
Franklin's mother, Sara Delano Roosevelt,
    was the daughter of a wealthy shipowner.
    Her family had come to America from
    France even before the Roosevelts arrived.

An early photograph of Franklin
Roosevelt, taken in February, 1883.

The Roosevelt home at Hyde Park.

Franklin on "Debby," his first pony.

Franklin was given almost everything a boy could want. He had his own pony at the family's Hyde Park estate.

He had his own sailboat at the family's summer home on Campobello Island, near the Maine coast. Sailing was his favorite sport. He also liked to swim, ice-skate, and play tennis.

His mother wanted to keep her only child with her as much as possible. Franklin studied at home, with teachers his parents hircd. He went with his parents on their trips to Europe.

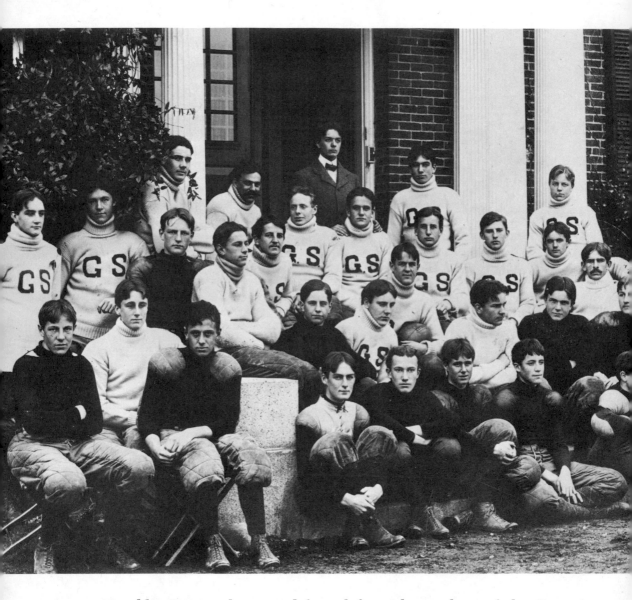

Franklin Roosevelt, second from left, with members of the Groton School football team, 1898.

When Franklin was fourteen he was sent to
Groton School — a boarding school for
wealthy boys. Two years later, the United
States went to war with Spain. Franklin
wanted to be a hero like his distant cousin
Theodore Roosevelt. "Teddy" Roosevelt led
the Rough Riders, a famous cavalry
regiment, in the war.

But Franklin caught scarlet fever. The brief
Spanish-American War was over before he
was well again.

In 1900, Franklin entered Harvard University. His father died soon afterward. His mother came to live near her son.

Franklin was not a brilliant student or a star athlete. He did not know what he wanted to do after his graduation. His mother wanted him to live the life of a wealthy gentleman at Hyde Park.

While at Harvard, Roosevelt (center) was the editor of the school news-paper, the *Harvard Crimson*.

Franklin with his father and mother, the year before his father died.

His father had always said that even a
   wealthy man should do some kind of
   useful work. Franklin thought his father
   had been right. He entered Columbia Law
   School.

Eleanor Roosevelt in her wedding gown, March 17, 1905.

Franklin was handsome and popular. He
went to many parties. Some of the parties
were at the White House.

His cousin Teddy Roosevelt had become
President. Teddy was a Republican. But
Franklin admired him very much even
though Franklin and his family were
Democrats. Franklin also admired the
President's shy niece, Eleanor Roosevelt.
He and Eleanor were married in 1905.

The two houses that were built for Franklin's mother, Sara Delano, at 47 and 49 East 65th Street, New York City

After Franklin finished law school he went to work for a New York law firm. His mother had two fine houses built in New York, side by side. One was for Franklin and Eleanor. The other was for herself. She managed both of them. Eleanor was too shy to stand up against her mother-in-law.

Eleanor read a great deal. She also spent a lot of time helping poor children. Once Eleanor took Franklin with her to a poor neighborhood. He had never seen real poverty before. He was shocked. He began to wonder if there was a way to cure it.

Eleanor helped Franklin start thinking about his real lifework. Many people say that marrying Eleanor was the wisest thing Franklin ever did.

Franklin made many speeches during the 1910 campaign.

In 1910, Democratic party leaders asked
Franklin to run for the New York state
senate. He agreed. Everyone was sure
Franklin would lose. Republicans had won
the senate seat in his district for 32 years.

The red Maxwell in which Franklin drove during the 1910 campaign.

Franklin rented a bright red car with big
brass headlights. It was one of the first
cars in his district. He drove it everywhere.
He talked to everyone. He shook hands.
He made speeches.
He won the election. He knew then that he
wanted to spend his life in politics.

Once he tried to run for the United States Senate without even telling the members of his party. They refused to support him. He was defeated. He discovered that he had to learn to work with other people, even if he did not always agree with them.

Franklin was still young and impatient. He often thought he knew more than the older leaders of his party. He had many quarrels with them.

Franklin on an inspection tour while Assistant Secretary of the Navy.

In 1912, Franklin worked hard for the election of President Woodrow Wilson. Wilson made Franklin his Assistant Secretary of the Navy.

Franklin did a good job. He helped to get the Navy in fighting shape for World War I.

Franklin accepting the nomination for Vice-President.

In 1920, Franklin was chosen as the
   Democratic candidate for Vice-President.
   He campaigned all over the country.
   Eleanor helped him.

He and Eleanor campaigned all over the country.

Franklin and his party lost the election. For the first time in ten years, Franklin was out of politics. While he waited for another chance to run for office, Franklin became a partner in a law firm. He also became a vice-president of an insurance company.

Suddenly, in the summer of 1921, he developed polio. This disease crippled hundreds of people every year. Franklin could not move his legs. They were paralyzed. The doctors said he would never walk again.

Most people were sure Franklin's political career was ended. His mother wanted him to live the quiet life of an invalid. But Eleanor reminded Franklin that only his legs were crippled — not his brain. She and his good friend and adviser Louis Howe kept him interested in politics.

Louis Howe.

Franklin was determined to bring strength back to his legs. Here, he
stands with the help of his doctor and an aide.

Franklin made up his mind that he did not want anyone to feel sorry for him. He learned to laugh at himself when people had to help him. He also tried hard to bring strength back to his crippled legs. He did painful exercises. He wore heavy steel leg braces.

Franklin in August, 1924, with John W. Davis.

He often swam at Warm Springs, Georgia.
He thought the warm waters there made
his legs stronger. He wanted other polio
victims to try the waters, too. With some
of his friends, he made Warm Springs a
treatment center for people crippled by
polio.

In 1924, Franklin was asked to speak at the
Democratic National Convention. Men
helped him out of his wheelchair. They
handed him his crutches. Thousands of
people watched him in silence.

Franklin started, alone, toward the speaker's
    desk. He took one slow step and then
    another. When he reached the desk he
    gripped it with both his strong hands.
    Then he lifted up his chin and grinned.
The crowd cheered. That day the Democrats
    knew they had found a new leader.
In 1928, Franklin was asked to run for
    governor of New York State. Many of his
    friends wanted him to refuse. Some
    believed that few Democrats could win
    that year, and that Franklin would be
    defeated. Others said the campaign would
    be too hard for someone who was crippled.

FDR taking the oath of office as governor of New York State.

But Franklin thought he could help his party
by running. He campaigned all over the
state. People gathered everywhere to hear
the fine speeches of "FDR," as they called
him.

FDR won the election.

The nation seemed prosperous that year.
Many people were growing rich buying
and selling shares on the stock market.

Then suddenly the price of stock market
shares fell. Rich men became poor
overnight. They stopped buying new cars
and clothes and other things.

People on relief waiting on line seeking jobs.

Stores went out of business. Factories had to
   close. Workers lost their jobs. Then they,
   too, stopped buying things — and more
   stores and factories shut down. The whole
   country was in a depression.

FDR carried out a program that helped the poor people of New York State. FDR thought the same kind of program should be carried out in the whole nation. He knew that the Republican President, Herbert Hoover, did not agree. FDR decided to try to become President himself.

He had to fight to win the Democratic nomination. He had to fight hard in his campaign, too. He told the voters that the Republicans had given workingmen a bad deal. He promised that his program would give them a New Deal.

FDR signing a bill in Albany, February 26, 1931.

FDR addressing the convention in Chicago in 1932.

FDR and his New Deal won the 1932
   election.
The most important idea behind FDR's New
   Deal was this: That the government
   should give jobs to people who were out
   of work. Then, FDR said, those people
   could afford to buy things again. Stores
   and factories would open once more. Soon
   people would be able to return to their
   old jobs. The depression would be over.
FDR asked Congress to pass new laws that
   would give him the power to carry out his
   program. Congress passed most of the
   laws he wanted.

The government hired these workers to build a playground.

The government hired thousands of people and put them to work. They built roads and bridges, schools and post offices. They planted trees. They painted pictures and performed plays.

Workers built dams like this one in Tennessee.

They built dams that stopped floods. Water flowing over some of those dams produced electric power. The government sold that power at low rates to farmers who had never had electricity before.

FDR made mistakes. Some parts of his program were not a success. But he was never afraid to give up a plan that did not work and try something new in its place. FDR made enemies, too. Some said he was trying to become more powerful than any President had the right to be.

Rich people complained about the new high
taxes. They said the President was taking
away their wealth and giving it to the
poor. They knew FDR was wealthy, too.
They called him a traitor to his own class.

But most voters thought FDR was helping
people to help themselves. They elected
him again in 1936 by a huge vote.

FDR during one of his famous "fireside chats" — radio broadcasts heard by Americans all over the country.

Americans also gave FDR a fine present.
Every year on his birthday they donated
dimes to help the victims of polio. They
called their present The March of Dimes.
World War II began in Europe during FDR's
second term. He wanted to help the
countries attacked by the armies of Italy
and Nazi Germany. There was not much
he could do. Most Americans wanted their
country to stay completely out of the war.
FDR did put scientists to work exploring the
atom. Several years later, those scientists
exploded the world's first atomic bomb.

Sara Delano, Eleanor, and FDR, driving to vote in the 1940 Presidential
election.

By 1940, FDR was sure the United States could not keep out of the war. He thought the country would need his experience as a leader in the years ahead. He said he would run for President again if his party wanted him.

No President had ever been elected to a third term. Some people said FDR wanted to become a dictator. Other people said FDR wanted to become President again so he could drag the United States into the war. FDR promised never to send Americans to fight in a foreign war. Once again, in 1940, he won the election.

By 1941, more Americans were willing to help fight Germany and Italy. Here, FDR signs the British Aid Bill.

By 1941 more Americans were willing to help fight Germany and Italy. They worked in factories to make guns and planes for England and Russia.

Before Congress, asking for the declaration of war.

On December 7, 1941, Japan attacked the United States naval base at Pearl Harbor, in Hawaii. FDR asked Congress to declare war on Japan. Congress did. Then Japan's allies, Germany and Italy, declared war on the United States.

World War II was no longer a foreign war. Now thousands of Americans joined the battle. American factories worked around the clock to turn out more guns and planes.

FDR was the first President to ever leave the country during wartime. He traveled thousands of miles to meet the leaders of England, Russia, and France. Together they made their battle plans.

Joseph Stalin, FDR, and Winston Churchill at a conference in Teheran, Iran, in 1943.

Eleanor and FDR receive their neighbors on election night, November 7, 1944.

The world leaders planned for peace, too.
They wanted to form an organization
strong enough to stop all future wars.
FDR suggested a name for it: the United
Nations.

The American people refused to change
their leader during the war. In 1944 they
elected FDR President for the fourth time.
By then the end of the war was in sight.
Victory for the United States and her allies
was not far off.

But FDR did not live to see the victory. The crippled President was worn out after twelve long years in office. He died suddenly in Warm Springs, Georgia, on the afternoon of April 12, 1945.

Millions of people in the United States and around the world mourned the death of Franklin Delano Roosevelt.

Mourners line the streets of Washington as the funeral procession approaches the Capitol Building.

# FRANKLIN DELANO ROOSEVELT

BORN: Hyde Park, New York, January 30, 1882. Son of James and Sara Delano Roosevelt.

EDUCATION: Groton School, Massachusetts, 1896-1900; Harvard University, 1900-1904; Columbia Law School, 1904-1907.

FAMILY: Wife, Anna Eleanor, married March 17, 1905. Children, Anna Eleanor, James, Elliott, Franklin Delano, Jr., John Aspinwall.

POSITIONS: State senator from Dutchess County, New York, 1911-1913; Assistant Secretary of the Navy, 1913-1920; governor of New York, 1929-1933; President of the United States, 1933-1945.